Original title:

Winter's Song

Author: Kaido Väinamäe

ISBN HARDBACK: 978-9908-1-1069-1

ISBN PAPERBACK: 978-9908-1-1070-7

ISBN EBOOK: 978-9908-1-1071-4

The Hearth's Warmth Against the Chill

In the glow of flames we gather near,
Laughter rising, filling the air.
Old tales shared with a friendly cheer,
Hearts grow warm as shadows dare.

Candles flicker, casting soft light,
Mirth and joy weave through the room.
Delicate whispers dance in the night,
Hope blooms brightly, banishing gloom.

Stockings hung with wishes and dreams,
Sweet scents waft from the kitchen's delight.
The clock invites magical themes,
As we revel through the starry night.

Snowflakes falling beyond the glass,
A silent world wrapped in white.
But here, in warmth, moments amass,
Hearts unite, glowing so bright.

Midnight's Silent Serenade

Beneath the stars, the whispers play,
Crickets sing in softest tones.
The moon bestows its silver ray,
As dreams awaken in tender zones.

A gathering of voices ring clear,
Together we cherish this tranquil night.
With laughter shared and joy sincere,
The world feels magic, everything right.

Echoes of music brush the dark,
Where shadows dance in a gentle sway.
Each note ignites a tender spark,
Leading our hearts in festive play.

Midnight joins in the celebration,
A symphony of love unfurled.
We find our peace, our jubilation,
As we embrace this wondrous world.

Quietude Beneath a Silver Sky

Soft whispers dance among the trees,
Laughter floats on a gentle breeze.
Candles flicker with warmth and cheer,
Under silver clouds, the night draws near.

Joyful hearts gather, voices blend,
Stories shared as time does bend.
Peaceful moments, the world feels right,
In quietude, we find pure delight.

Twilight's Embrace in Frost

Twilight drapes in hues of blue,
Frosty air with a magical view.
Stars blink softly, their twinkle bright,
Covering the world in a blanket of light.

Children play in the crisp night air,
Breath of wonder ignites the fair.
With every laugh, a melody sung,
In twilight's embrace, we feel forever young.

Beneath Layers of Snow

Blankets of white on fields so wide,
Where laughter echoes and dreams reside.
Snowflakes tumble, a graceful fall,
Each one unique, a wonder for all.

Hot cocoa waits, a treat so sweet,
By the fire, we gather, hearts feel the beat.
Wrapped in warmth, as stories unfold,
Beneath layers of snow, memories are gold.

Breath of the Icy Owl

In the stillness of a winter's night,
An icy owl takes glorious flight.
With wings spread wide, it soars up high,
Guarding secrets under the starry sky.

Moonlight glimmers on restful trees,
Whispers of joy carried by the breeze.
We marvel together, a festive sight,
As nature's wonders fill the night.

A Glimmer in the Frost

In morning's light, the frost does gleam,
A dance of stars, a winter's dream.
The laughter echoes in the air,
As joy and warmth break through despair.

The trees adorned in sparkling white,
A wonderland in pure delight.
We gather close, our spirits rise,
In this sweet chill, our hearts surprise.

The Last Breath of Autumn

Leaves will twirl in the gentle breeze,
Copper and gold, a sight to please.
Gathered friends, with mugs in hand,
We whisper tales, a cozy band.

The harvest moons bring laughter near,
Of thanks and joy, we hold so dear.
A final cheer for summer's end,
In every smile, a love to send.

Gazing at the Shimmering Night

Beneath a cloak of velvet skies,
The stars ignite, a dance that flies.
With every twinkle, dreams take flight,
In wonder wrapped, we greet the night.

A fire crackles, warmth surrounds,
In every laugh, pure joy resounds.
With hearts aglow, we sing so bright,
Together we bask in this delight.

Illusions of Warmth

Candles flicker with a soft embrace,
In glowing shadows, we find our place.
The scent of spices fills the cold,
With stories shared, new joys unfold.

Embracing hugs and whispered cheer,
The world outside feels far, unclear.
In this cocoon of laughter's bloom,
We chase away the winter's gloom.

Cascades of Quietude

Whispers dance on winter's breeze,
Glistening flakes twirl with ease.
Softly falling, a gentle grace,
Nature's hush in this sacred space.

Candles flicker, shadows play,
Golden warmth in hearts today.
Joyful laughter fills the air,
A festive spirit everywhere.

The Breath of Frigid Air

Crystal branches reach for light,
Shimmer in the starry night.
Chilled winds carry songs so bright,
Melodies of pure delight.

Gathered close, friends share their dreams,
Laughter mixed with soft moonbeams.
Hearts aglow, a timeless cheer,
In this moment, love is near.

Chime of Crystal Clarity

Bells resound, a joyful sound,
In this wonder, peace is found.
Snowflakes swirl like dreams anew,
Every moment sparkles true.

Warmth of hearts, a festive call,
Together we shall rise and fall.
Under stars, our spirits soar,
In this magic, we want more.

Underneath the Frosted Canopy

Underneath a blanket white,
Whispers twinkle, pure delight.
Branches heavy, covered bright,
Nature's canvas shines at night.

Gather round the crackling fire,
Voices lift, our souls inspire.
In this moment, we are one,
Celebrating 'till the day is done.

The Glimmer of Icy Stars

Under the bright and frosty skies,
Glimmers twinkle, joy flies high.
Snowflakes dance in chilly air,
Whispers of magic everywhere.

Children laugh, their spirits light,
Building dreams in purest white.
Candles glow with warmth and cheer,
As festive songs ring loud and clear.

Whispers Beneath the Frozen Lake

Beneath the ice, where secrets lie,
Whispers of joy float softly by.
Laughter weaves through the trees,
A melody carried on the winter breeze.

Skaters glide with hearts aglow,
Their movements weave a lovely show.
As stars above in the night sky,
Reflect the dreams of days gone by.

Embrace of the Polar Moon

The polar moon, so bright and bold,
Watches over tales of old.
Frosted branches gently sway,
In the soft light of the play.

Nature wraps in snowy shawl,
As joyful voices rise and call.
Beneath her gaze, we gather near,
To celebrate the time of year.

Slumbering Earth in White

The earth in slumber, soft and white,
Cradles dreams in the cold night.
A blanket thick, a peaceful rest,
Nature's heart beats in its chest.

With every flake that gently falls,
A symphony of winter calls.
Hearts unite in snowflakes' dance,
In this season, we find romance.

The Edge of Solitude

In the quiet night, laughter rings,
Bright lanterns sway on silver strings.
Hearts ignite like stars in flight,
Together we dance till morning light.

Friends gather round, stories unfold,
Joyous memories, shimmering gold.
Voices echo, a melodic cheer,
Let the spirit of festivity steer.

With each twirl, worries drift away,
In this moment, we choose to play.
Time pauses, embracing the glow,
At the edge of solitude, love starts to flow.

Cloaked in Frost

A blanket of white on the world below,
Each breath a whisper, gentle and slow.
Kids in the yard, with snowflakes to chase,
Laughter ignites in the frosty embrace.

Hot cocoa steaming in mugs held tight,
Fond memories bloom in the chilly night.
Carols drift softly, a harmonious thread,
As twinkling lights sparkle overhead.

Wrapped in our warmth, under blankets spread,
We share in the stories, the words we've said.
Cloaked in frost, our hearts stay near,
In this festive cheer, we've nothing to fear.

The Weight of a Snowflake

Delicate dance from the heavens above,
Each snowflake falls, a sign of our love.
A gentle touch on a waiting ground,
In their soft landing, joy can be found.

Children leap in the drifts piled high,
Making snow angels beneath the sky.
With every swirl, imagination soars,
The weight of a snowflake, opening doors.

As night descends, the world glows bright,
Each shimmering flake, a wish in flight.
Around the hearth, stories are spun,
In the embrace of winter, we are all one.

Shadows Cast by Liquid Gold

Sunset whispers in hues bold and bright,
As the day bows down, welcoming night.
The glow of lanterns dances with grace,
Shadows cast by liquid gold fill the space.

Laughter spills softly, a magical sound,
In the heart of the moment, joy is unbound.
Festive feasts laid out with delight,
Friends gathered close, a beautiful sight.

Together we share in the warmth of the glow,
Creating memories that linger and flow.
In this shimmering night, our spirits unfold,
As shadows are drawn, we cherish the gold.

Hibernal Reflections

Snowflakes dance upon the breeze,
Joyful hearts, the world at ease.
Firelight flickers, warmth bestowed,
In winter's arms, our hopes unload.

Laughter echoes, candles bright,
Friends together, pure delight.
A feast of flavors, love's embrace,
Memories made in this bright space.

Starlit skies, so vast and clear,
Each twinkle holds a wish sincere.
Embrace the moment, time stands still,
In hibernal joy, we find our will.

Delicate Crystals in the Air

Delicate crystals fall from trees,
Glistening softly in the freeze.
Children giggle, their breaths in clouds,
Bundled in scarves, they join the crowds.

Lights are strung on every lane,
Colors bright, a sweet refrain.
Hot cocoa sipped by the glow,
Warmth inside, as love will flow.

Songs of cheer drift through the night,
Festive spirits taking flight.
Under moonlit skies so rare,
Together we find joy to share.

Frostbitten Lullabies

Frostbitten branches sway and hum,
Soft lullabies of winter's drum.
The world adorned in silver lace,
A tranquil, peaceful, tender space.

Beneath the stars, we gather near,
Whispers of dreams, a time to cheer.
Each breath a cloud, in night's embrace,
Carols sung, with a warm grace.

Sparkling snow underfoot we tread,
Stories shared, our spirits fed.
In frosty air, our hearts unite,
Frostbitten joys, a pure delight.

Whispers in the Frosted Pines

Whispers play among the pines,
Tales of warmth, as daylight shines.
Frosted needles, nature's art,
Each breath fills up the hopeful heart.

Glistening fields, a wondrous sight,
Sunrise paints the world in light.
Families gather, laughter rings,
In harmony, our spirits sing.

Gather 'round the crackling fire,
One by one, our tales inspire.
In the crisp air, joy ignites,
Whispers turn to festive nights.

Enduring the Quiet

In the stillness of frosty nights,
Laughter dances in the moon's glow,
Stars twinkle like joyful lights,
Whispers of warmth, a soothing flow.

Joyful hearts gather near,
Embracing the chill with delight,
Songs of friendship fill the air,
Hoping to last through the night.

Snowflakes twirl in a playful race,
Wrapping us up in their soft embrace,
Stories shared in the crackling fire,
Invoking dreams that never tire.

With every cheer, the silence breaks,
Harmony sings in every laugh,
Echoes of joy the winter makes,
Together we forge our warming path.

The Resilient Heart of Cold

Frosty petals on window panes,
A crisp breeze carries light cheer,
Beneath the snow, life still remains,
Hope thrives strong, passionate and clear.

Gathered close in winter's embrace,
Hands entwined against the cold,
Glimmers of love, warmth we trace,
With every moment, memories unfold.

The heart beats loud through icy air,
Resilient like the sun's bright beam,
Beneath the layers of chilly care,
We find the strength, we find the dream.

Songs of joy, echo round and round,
Footprints leading to open doors,
With laughter's warmth, we are unbound,
In this quiet, our spirit soars.

A Chorus for the Shivering

Gather 'round, it's time to sing,
Voices blend like the frost and fire,
Merriment in every offering,
From whispers soft to hearts aspire.

Jingle bells ring through the night,
A symphony of winter's call,
In every note, the pure delight,
Warmth awaits, we share it all.

Hands uplifted, spirits soar,
Under stars, twinkling as we sway,
Unity echoes from shore to shore,
Igniting the joy of a festive day.

With every cheer, a fire ignites,
Melodies chase away the gloom,
Within the heart, the love ignites,
Together we blossom, we bloom.

Melodies of Icicles

Draped in wonder, icicles gleam,
Nature's music, a crystal band,
Each drop plays out a winter dream,
Echoes wrap around our land.

The air is fresh, alive with cheer,
Soft laughter ringing, bright and clear,
Footprints crunch in the snow so white,
Every moment feels so right.

Beneath the branches, laughter reigns,
Gifts of joy, wrapped in the sun,
Celebrating through frosty lanes,
Under the sky, we are all one.

Festive spirits quicken our pace,
In the glow of the twinkling lights,
Together we cherish this embrace,
A chorus of warmth ignites the nights.

Muffled Footsteps in the Snow

Softly falls the white blanket,
Footprints whisper on the ground.
Laughter dances in the cold,
Joyful echoes all around.

Snowflakes twirl in the air,
Children sing with pure delight.
Mittens hug their tiny hands,
Snowmen bask in glowing light.

Sleds are racing down the hill,
Hot cocoa warms our hands so tight.
Stars above begin to shine,
Celebration through the night.

Winter's magic fills the sky,
Every heart beats in a glow.
Muffled footsteps in the snow,
A tapestry of joy to sew.

The Touch of a Cold Breeze

Through the trees, a whisper blows,
A cold breeze brings the festive cheer.
With every rustle, laughter grows,
As warmth prevails, drawing us near.

Scarves are wrapped around our necks,
Lively songs fill up the night.
Under string lights, hearts connect,
In this season, spirits bright.

The moon hangs low, all aglow,
Each breath puffs like a tiny cloud.
Chasing dreams in soft, white snow,
Together, we stand warm and proud.

With the touch of a cold breeze,
Nature bows, a dance of grace.
Joyful hearts, we find our ease,
In this wonderland, our place.

A Story Told in Snowdrifts

Once upon a frosty eve,
Stories twinkle in the night.
Snowdrifts tell of love and dreams,
Underneath the soft moonlight.

Warmth resides in hearts aglow,
Every tale a spark of light.
Candles flicker, embers flow,
Carried high in the starry sight.

Footprints trace the paths we've wandered,
In each twist, new joys unfold.
Laughter lingers, ever pondered,
A story told in hugs and gold.

Gathered close, friends by the fire,
Sharing tales both old and new.
In this season, our hearts inspire,
A tapestry of joy enfused.

Lanterns in the Gloom

Flickering lights in the dark,
Lanterns sway, casting soft beams.
With every spark, we leave a mark,
Crafting wishes, chasing dreams.

In the chill, our laughter rings,
Every moment shines so bright.
Voices join, as the music sings,
Clutching warmth in the starry night.

Together here, our spirits soar,
Amidst the glow, we find our way.
Creating memories, wanting more,
In this festivity's sweet ballet.

Lanterns lift our hearts in gloom,
In unity, we dare to believe.
As the night begins to bloom,
It's in this joy, we truly weave.

Icebound Reverie

In twilight's glow, the icebergs gleam,
Serenades of snowflakes dance, it seems.
Whispers of joy in the crisp, cold air,
Laughter and love are everywhere.

Glowing lanterns twinkle through the night,
Mittens and scarves wrap hearts so tight.
Families gather, united and warm,
Creating memories that forever charm.

A Canvas of White

Blanketed fields in majestic white,
Children tumble with pure delight.
Snowmen rise with hats set askew,
Pine trees adorn whispers of dew.

Cocoa brews with a hint of cheer,
A symphony plays, sweet to the ear.
Fireplaces crackle, stories unfold,
Wonders of winter, timeless and bold.

The Poetry of Icy Stillness

In the stillness, a soft hush prevails,
Frostbite kisses on cheeks, like fairy tales.
Stars shine brighter in the winter night,
Each twinkle a promise, each glow a light.

Moonlit paths glisten, quiet and bright,
Nature adorned in her finest white.
Joy lingers long in the snowy embrace,
A tapestry woven in time and space.

Frostbitten Sunrises

Golden hues break the icy dawn,
Paint the world where dreams are drawn.
Frosted branches twinkle and sway,
Signaling the birth of a festive day.

Scarves wrapped tight, we venture outside,
Chasing shadows where warmth will collide.
The air is crisp, with laughter so bright,
A frosty morning, pure festive delight.

A Dance of Snowflakes

Snowflakes twirl in frosty air,
Whispers soft, like a gentle prayer.
Laughter echoes through the night,
Joyful hearts in pure delight.

Children dash with glee and cheer,
Building dreams, the magic near.
Glowing lights on trees aglow,
Shimmering paths where wishes flow.

Scarves wrapped tight, hands hold warm mugs,
Stories shared, with joyful hugs.
The world embraced in winter's art,
A festive rhythm, heart to heart.

The Stillness Between Storms

A hush falls down, the world at peace,
Between the storms, a sweet release.
Gentle breezes stir the pines,
Nature hums, in quiet signs.

Footsteps soft on snow-clad ground,
In this still, a joy is found.
Dancing shadows play and dart,
As the light ignites the heart.

Gathered round, friends share a glow,
Warmth of laughter, ebb and flow.
In this pause, our spirits soar,
A festive calm we all adore.

Dreams in a Silver Gleam

Moonlight glimmers on the snow,
A silken dance, a soft aglow.
Whispers of dreams float through the night,
Festive magic, pure delight.

Children's laughter fills the sky,
Snowmen grinning, standing high.
Under stars, we share our dreams,
In this world, nothing's as it seems.

Firelight crackles with a song,
Friends united, where we belong.
Every moment, cherished, bright,
A silver gleam, a joyous sight.

Frost-Kissed Melodies

Frosted branches, crystals shine,
Nature's canvas, so divine.
Through the air, sweet songs we send,
Harmony with every friend.

Carols float on chilly breeze,
Winter magic, hearts at ease.
In the glow of lantern's light,
We embrace the starry night.

Pies and treats all laid with care,
Sharing moments, love to share.
In this time, our spirits rise,
Frost-kissed melodies fill the skies.

The Subtle Art of Silence

In the hush of twilight's kiss,
Whispers dance upon the breeze.
Candles glow in warm embrace,
Silent laughter, hearts at ease.

Snowflakes waltz from sky to ground,
Each a gem that softly sighs.
Muffled joy in every sound,
Where the spirit softly flies.

Amidst the stillness, love is found,
Gentle echoes fill the air.
Magic twinkles all around,
In the moments that we share.

A Tapestry of Ice

Glistening threads of frosty white,
Weave a quilt of pure delight.
Stars are stitched in velvet night,
Each a dream in silver light.

Children laugh, they spin and glide,
On this frozen tapestry.
Joy and wonder, side by side,
Crafting memories, wild and free.

Carols ring through chilly air,
Notes of love and peace combine.
In this moment, hearts declare,
Life is sweet, and all is fine.

Nocturnal Secrets of the Cold

Under stars that wink and glow,
Secrets whisper 'neath the snow.
Every shadow, every light,
Holds a tale of sheer delight.

Fires crackle with a cheer,
Hot cocoa warms both heart and hand.
In the night, the world feels near,
Wrapped in warmth, together we stand.

Laughter echoes through the trees,
As the moon invites our play.
In the cold, our hearts find ease,
Sharing stories, come what may.

The Heartbeat of the Hearth

In the glow of flickering flames,
Families gather, passing grace.
Joyful voices, all the same,
In this sacred, cherished space.

Sweet aromas fill the air,
Home-cooked meals and laughter shared.
Love is found everywhere,
In these moments, hearts declared.

With each heartbeat, time stands still,
Embraced by warmth, both near and far.
In this haven, spirits thrill,
Together beneath the evening star.

Sledding Down Memory Lane

We race down slopes with joyful shouts,
The crisp, cold air spinning about.
Laughter dances on winter's breath,
In golden moments, we find depth.

Snowflakes twirl like dreams in flight,
As children play in pure delight.
Each curve brings joy, sharp and bright,
Together we sled, hearts feel light.

The sound of crunch, the whoosh of speed,
In every push, we plant a seed.
Of memories made, of smiles shared,
In frosty fun, we are all paired.

So let us sled and chase the sun,
Our winter tales have just begun.
With every run, our spirits soar,
Sledding down lanes we can't ignore.

The Last Leaf on a Bare Tree

A solitary leaf clings tight,
With colors bold against the night.
Its beauty shines, though chill is near,
A beacon bright, a sign of cheer.

Under skies painted shades of gray,
It flutters gently, swaying, sway.
Amidst the cold, it stands so proud,
A fragile, golden beauty loud.

As winter whispers, softly sings,
The memory of warmth it brings.
Though all around may seem so stark,
It holds the summer's glowing spark.

So let us pause to share this view,
The last leaf clings, our hearts anew.
In every season, hope does weave,
A tapestry of dreams we believe.

Chasing Shadows in the Chill

Amidst the frost and fading light,
We chase the shadows, hearts so bright.
Each corner turned brings laughter loud,
In winter's grip, we feel so proud.

Our breath a mist, our spirits free,
In snowy fields, pure ecstasy.
We run and play, no care in sight,
Creating warmth in the brisk night.

The chill wraps close, but we don't mind,
With every step, new joys we find.
Together dancing in the glow,
Of moonlit trails and flurries slow.

So join the chase, let laughter swell,
In winter's grip, we'll cast a spell.
For in these moments, clear and still,
We find our joy, our hearts to fill.

Tea by the Fire

With steaming cups and dancing flames,
We share our stories, laugh, and games.
The crackling wood, a soothing song,
In cozy warmth, where we belong.

The winter winds may howl and moan,
But here in peace, we're not alone.
With every sip, the world feels right,
As shadows flicker in soft light.

The aroma swirls, a fragrant bliss,
Each moment cherished, none to miss.
We toast to warmth, to bonds so true,
With every mug, my heart sings too.

So let us gather, friends so dear,
With tales and tea, we have no fear.
By the fire's glow, our spirits lift,
In simple moments, life's greatest gift.

Crystal Serenade

In the evening's glow, we dance,
Under stars that twinkle, a vibrant trance.
With laughter rising like bubbles of cheer,
We gather close, loved ones near.

Candles flicker, casting warm light,
Joyful hearts celebrate through the night.
Songs of old weave through the air,
Harmony echoes, free of despair.

Gifts wrapped with care, tied with a bow,
Moments shared in the soft, gentle snow.
Glasses raised for the spirits we toast,
To friendship and laughter, the ones we love most.

As the night unfolds with festive sound,
In this moment of magic, bliss is found.
May the joy linger as seasons unfold,
In the Crystal Serenade, memories gold.

Hibernal Reverie

The world wrapped in a snowy embrace,
Each flake a whisper, each drift a trace.
Under moonlight, dreams softly play,
In the warmth of togetherness, we sway.

Cocoa steaming, marshmallows afloat,
Stories retold by the fire's note.
With each click of the clock, time slows down,
In this hibernal bliss, we wear love's crown.

Beneath the blankets, laughter ignites,
Sharing secrets on chilly nights.
The warmth of your smile, a winter's delight,
As the stars twinkle, shining so bright.

Wrapped in the magic of this season's tune,
To the rhythm of hearts, we dance with the moon.
In the Hibernal Reverie, peace we embrace,
As dreams intertwine in this cozy space.

The Frost's Lullaby

Gentle whispers of winter's breath,
Each moment a gift, cherished like wealth.
Frosty patterns on the windowpane,
Nature's artwork, a beautiful gain.

Candles flicker with warm, soft light,
In the hush of the evening, all feels right.
Songs of the season fill up the air,
In the glow of the candles, we banish despair.

Children giggle, bundled in scarves,
Creating snowmen, warming our hearts.
Together we sing, our voices unite,
In the Frost's Lullaby, joy takes flight.

With every note of this enchanting song,
We find our place where we all belong.
As the season wraps us in shimmering white,
The Frost's Lullaby beckons us to delight.

Gleaming Shadows on Ice

Beneath the moon, the ice glistens bright,
Gleaming shadows chase dreams through the night.
Skates carve patterns, laughter resonates,
In this magical space, joy elevates.

The crisp winter air fills up our lungs,
While heartwarming melodies drift like songs.
Hand in hand as we glide and play,
In this festival of light, we find our way.

Colorful lights shimmer on frozen streets,
Each step we take, the world's music beats.
In this winter wonder, we lose track of time,
Under the stars, our spirits climb.

As the night deepens, hearts intertwine,
In all of this magic, we feel divine.
Gleaming Shadows on Ice, a sight to behold,
Binding us together in stories untold.

Echoes in the Crystal Caverns

In caverns bright, laughter rings,
As friends unite and joy it brings.
With glimmering lights that dance and play,
Echoes of cheer fill up the day.

Stalactites shimmer in festive hues,
Mirrored reflections, a wondrous view.
Voices soar through the chilly air,
Bound by the magic, we all share.

In the depths where secrets hide,
We gather 'round, our hearts open wide.
Celebration flows like a gentle stream,
In crystal caverns, we dare to dream.

Here where the light and laughter blend,
We cherish moments with family and friend.
In every echo, a story to tell,
In this enchanted realm, we all dwell.

The Flicker of Candlelight

Candle flames dance in joyous glee,
Casting shadows, wild and free.
With every flicker, a secret shared,
Moments of peace, tenderly spared.

Gather 'round, let your spirits soar,
In the warm glow, there's always more.
Whispers of love float through the night,
As hearts unite in the candlelight.

Wishes are made on this festive eve,
Traces of joy in the air we breathe.
Songs arise, with laughter entwined,
In the flicker, sweet memories bind.

In the twilight, dreams take flight,
As the world outside fades from sight.
Hearts aglow in this gentle embrace,
With candlelight's warmth, we find our place.

The Scent of Pine in Snow

Amidst the woods, a wondrous found,
The scent of pine in snowy ground.
Branches glisten with a silver layer,
Nature adorns, a festive player.

Footfalls crunch on the frozen floor,
With laughter echoing, none ignore.
In winter's hush, our hearts ignite,
Under the moon, the world feels right.

Adorned trees with stars so bright,
Whispers of wonder fill the night.
As snowflakes twirl in a joyous spin,
We embrace the magic that lies within.

With every breath, the pinewood sings,
A symphony of peace that winter brings.
In this moment, we all belong,
Bound by joy, where hearts grow strong.

Footprints in the Fresh Powder

In winter's canvas, pure and white,
Footprints trace paths in soft moonlight.
Laughter follows in frosty trails,
As friends embark on snowy gales.

Each step taken, a thrill anew,
Creating memories as we pursue.
With snowballs flying and cheer in the air,
In every laugh, a moment to share.

Bundle up tight, let the warmth spread,
With hot cocoa dreams and smiles ahead.
The world feels bright with each playful bound,
Footprints together, our joy profound.

As stars twinkle in the evening shade,
In fresh powder, our adventures laid.
Together we roam, through winter's reign,
In joyous spirits, we dance through the grain.

Fur-Lined Dreams

In the glow of twinkling lights,
Laughter dances through the night.
Snowflakes flutter, soft and fair,
Joyful hearts in winter's care.

Cocoa warms our dreaming souls,
Fur-lined whispers, magic rolls.
Under stars, we share our dreams,
Wrapped in love, or so it seems.

Candles flicker, shadows play,
Sparkling eyes that light the way.
With every hug and every cheer,
The spirit of this time is clear.

Songs of joy, so sweetly sung,
Underneath the snowflakes flung.
With a dreamy, warm embrace,
Festive smiles, our hearts we lace.

Nightfall's Gentle Caress

Nightfall's caress, a silken touch,
The world slows down, it means so much.
Stars emerge in velvet skies,
Underneath their watchful eyes.

Families gather, stories weave,
Laughter echoes, hearts believe.
Deck the halls with lights so bright,
In this season's pure delight.

The air is thick with joy and glee,
Gift-wrapped secrets wait for thee.
Moonlight dances on the ground,
In this magic, love is found.

A time for giving, warmth, and cheer,
Embrace the moments, hold them near.
As nightfall wraps its gentle arms,
Festive spirit, all its charms.

Frosted Whispers of Twilight

Frosted whispers in the air,
Wardrobe trimmed with sparkle rare.
Twilight settles, hush so sweet,
Magic echoes with each heartbeat.

Carols sung by candlelight,
Filling hearts with pure delight.
Gifts of kindness, wrapped with care,
Gentle memories we all share.

Playful snowflakes swirling down,
Adorning every joyful town.
Underneath the starry glow,
Festive cheer begins to flow.

In winter's warmth, we find our way,
Gather 'round, let's laugh and play.
Together here, our spirits soar,
Frosted whispers, we adore.

The Tale of the Snowbound

In the hush of a snowbound night,
Dreams take flight in pure starlight.
Stories shared by the fire's glow,
Warmth and laughter, hearts aglow.

Blankets piled, snug and tight,
The world outside, a pure white sight.
Together we weave the tales of old,
In this season, our hearts unfold.

Cup in hand, we share a toast,
For every friend we cherish most.
Magic sparkles in the air,
In winter's arms, love is rare.

As morning greets the soft sunrise,
The world awakes with joyous sighs.
In every heart, the story's found,
A festive warmth in the snowbound.

Chill of the Silent Night

Stars twinkle bright in the velvet sky,
Families gather, laughter is nigh.
Candles flicker, the warmth fills the air,
Joyful hearts glow as love we share.

Outside the windows, the snowflakes dance,
Carols echo, and children prance.
Mistletoe hangs, a spark in the night,
Under its charm, everything feels right.

The chill in the air, but spirits run high,
Wishes are whispered; they drift and fly.
Hope is alive in each heartfelt song,
In this festive moment, we all belong.

Frosted Whispers

In the frosty dawn, the world glistens bright,
Wrapped in warm layers, we step into light.
Cup of hot cocoa, fingers entwined,
Each moment cherished, our hearts aligned.

Snowflakes are falling like whispers of cheer,
The chill in the air brings loved ones near.
With every laughter, our worries take flight,
Together we shine on this magical night.

Fireside stories, as shadows engage,
We share dreams and hopes on life's festive stage.
The frosted delights and the joyous embrace,
Fill the room with warmth, a comforting space.

Echoes of the Frozen Breeze

Echoes of laughter, a festive refrain,
In the crisp air, not a shadow of pain.
The sight of the snowfall, so pure and divine,
Brings memories near, like a well-aged wine.

Candles aglow, every flicker speaks tales,
Of seasons gone by where joy never pales.
Underneath stars, we dance in delight,
With echoes of love wrapping warm through the night.

Chiming of bells in the heart of the town,
As music surrounds and spins us around.
With family and friends, we raise a cheer high,
In the echoes of laughter, the spirit will fly.

Beneath the Snowy Veil

Beneath the snowy veil, the world feels anew,
Colors of warmth in the crisp morning dew.
With every soft flake, there's magic at play,
Uniting our hearts in a festive bouquet.

Gifts exchanged under sparkling lights,
Filled with sweet laughter and joy that ignites.
Hot cider bubbling, the air filled with glee,
As friends gather 'round, sharing cups of pure tea.

The charm of the season, it wraps us so tight,
Creating a canvas of pure winter white.
Every smile shared ignites the cold air,
Beneath the snowy veil, love is everywhere.

The Hush of a Snowbound Dream

In silence fall the snowflakes white,
Each twirl and spin, a joyful sight.
The world is wrapped in gleaming light,
A hush that feels so pure and bright.

Children laugh with pure delight,
They build a snowman, such a height.
With rosy cheeks, hearts take flight,
In dreams of magic, all feels right.

The evening glows with lights aglow,
As crisp air whispers, soft and slow.
Inside, warmth spreads like melted snow,
In this sweet peace, time seems to slow.

The stars above, they twinkle rare,
While love and joy are everywhere.
In every heart, a festive flare,
A snowbound dream, we freely share.

Tapestry of Chill and Glow

The night wraps us in velvet dark,
With flickering flames that softly spark.
A tapestry of light and chill,
Each whispered joy, a festive thrill.

Candles dance with shadows long,
In joyous echoes, we belong.
With every laugh, our spirits rise,
A chorus sung under starlit skies.

The air is filled with sweet delight,
As families gather, hearts so bright.
With treats and games, the laughter flows,
In this warm glow, our love just grows.

Let every moment weave a thread,
In this wild fabric, love is spread.
'Tis a night of peace, a wondrous show,
This tapestry of chill and glow.

Frost on the Windowpane

Frost adorns each pane with art,
Nature's brush, a splendid start.
The world transformed, a crystal scene,
Where winter weaves its magic sheen.

Inside, the warmth of laughter rings,
As joy abounds and spirit sings.
With hot cocoa, we toast the night,
In cozy corners, everything's right.

Outside, the world in silver drapes,
Each flake a dance, as winter shapes.
Through frosted glass, the moonlight glows,
A magical realm, where wonder flows.

With friends gathered near, we share our dreams,
In this frosty world, nothing's as it seems.
A festive spirit forever remains,
In the beauty of frost on the windowpane.

Whispering Winds of Chill

The winds are whispering softly now,
With every breath, they take a bow.
A chill envelops the night air,
Yet warmth of friends is everywhere.

Laughter dances through the trees,
As joy spills out upon the breeze.
With every note of winter's song,
In unity, we all belong.

The stars above twinkle bright,
Guiding us through this festive night.
In whispered dreams, hopes take flight,
As hearts beat strong with pure delight.

Let the winds of chill embrace,
A cozy feeling fills this space.
In every hug, and every cheer,
The festive whispers draw us near.

The Silence of Snowflakes

Falling softly, pure and white,
A blanket of peace, pure delight.
Whispers dance on winter's breath,
Embracing warmth, defying death.

Laughter echoes, children play,
Building dreams in soft array.
Hot cocoa warms the chilly hands,
Joy unfolds, as friendship stands.

Glistening lights on branches bright,
Stars above in festive night.
Carols sung with hearts aglow,
In this moment, spirits flow.

Memories made, with cheer and grace,
Every smile, a warm embrace.
The silence wrapped in snowy peace,
A time for love that will not cease.

Echoes of a Frozen Dawn

Morning breaks in hues of gold,
Each ray a story, warm yet bold.
Gentle breezes, crisp and sweet,
Nature's dance, a rhythmic beat.

Footsteps crunch on frosty ground,
In every sound, pure joy is found.
Gathered friends in playful cheer,
Happiness is drawing near.

Snowmen smile with coal-black eyes,
Underneath the azure skies.
Gathered close, our voices rise,
In laughter bright, dreams realize.

The winter sun, a golden crown,
Embracing all in this small town.
Memories woven, hearts entwined,
In frozen dawn, true joy we find.

Hushed Conversations in the Cold

Under blankets, stories shared,
Silent moments, love declared.
Warmth and laughter fill the air,
In this space, we lay our care.

Hands hold mugs of steaming cheer,
With every sip, we draw near.
Outside, snowflakes swirl and spin,
Inside, warmth is where we begin.

Tales of old, and dreams anew,
Each word a bond, our spirits grew.
The chill outside only brings
A festive mood, as warmth it sings.

In hushed tones, we celebrate,
Gathered close, we navigate.
In this cozy, winter fold,
Whispers linger, stories told.

Frost-Kissed Memories

Once upon a frosty night,
Stars above, the world so bright.
Laughter echoes, sweet and clear,
Together always, those we hold dear.

Lanes adorned with twinkling lights,
Filling hearts with pure delights.
Each step a dance on snowy trails,
In every breath, the spirit prevails.

Crisp air thick with hopes and dreams,
Through frosty windows, joy redeems.
Gather around with song and cheer,
In every heartbeat, love draws near.

Time may pass, but we will find,
Frost-kissed memories, intertwined.
In every season, love will bloom,
Festival brightens every room.

Starlit Chill Over Empty Streets

Beneath the twinkling, velvet sky,
Whispers dance as shadows sigh.
Lanterns flicker, spirits bright,
In the stillness, hearts take flight.

Snowflakes fall like gentle dreams,
Muffled laughter softly beams.
Each rooftop wears a crystal crown,
In this magic, joy is found.

Footsteps crunch on frosty ground,
Echoes of the night abound.
Stars above our hopes ignite,
Wrapped in warmth, we share delight.

In the chill, love's warmth we trace,
In twilight's hug, we find our place.
Together in this silvery glow,
Festive tales of peace we sow.

The Lullaby of the Longest Night

Moonlight spills on silent trees,
A gentle hush carries on the breeze.
Whispers linger, stories shared,
In this moment, hearts are bared.

Candles flicker, spirits near,
Melodies of joy and cheer.
Wrapped in warmth, we hum along,
Finding solace in our song.

Stars above like diamonds shine,
Woven closely, yours and mine.
In the night, our dreams take flight,
As we dance in pure delight.

The longest shadows fade away,
Celebrating night, welcoming day.
With every breath, we weave the light,
In this lullaby, we share the night.

A Blanket of Stillness

A blanket of snow, pure and white,
Covers the world in soft twilight.
Sparkling crystals on every bough,
Nature whispers, 'Come join now.'

Laughter rings out from hidden lanes,
As joy bursts forth from winter's chains.
Snowmen stand with carrot noses,
In this realm where magic dozes.

Hot cocoa warms our frosted hands,
While festive cheer unites all the lands.
Around the fire, stories unfold,
In this season, our hearts are bold.

The blanket thick, a soft embrace,
Underneath, we find our place.
Together beneath the starry night,
In stillness, we bask in the light.

Glimmers of Icy Light

Glimmers dance on frozen lakes,
As twilight whispers, the silence wakes.
Icicles shimmer, a crystal choir,
In this chill, we feel the fire.

Frosted branches, twinkling bright,
Breathe in deep the crisp, clear night.
With every sparkle, dreams take flight,
As hearts unite in pure delight.

Snowflakes drift in gentle sway,
Reminding us that joy's the way.
Together we sing with all our might,
In this world of icy light.

The moon rises, casting its spell,
In this moment, all is well.
Glimmers spark in every heart,
A festive night, we won't depart.

Beneath a Shroud of White

Snowflakes twirl and spin in glee,
Lending the world a soft, bright sheet.
Children laugh, their cheeks aglow,
Beneath a shroud of white, stars bestow.

Footprints crunch on winter's floor,
Echoes of joy through a cozy door.
Hot cocoa swirls in mugs so warm,
While fires crackle, hearts keep calm.

Laughter dances with chilly air,
Spreading warmth with love to spare.
Lights twinkle like diamonds fair,
A tapestry of joy beyond compare.

Gathered close, we count our dreams,
In snowy silence, life redeems.
Beneath a shroud, together we sway,
In this festive night, all fears melt away.

A Fire's Flicker Against the Dark

In the hearth, a fire's glow,
Crackles softly, casting low.
Shadows dance on walls around,
Magic whispers, warmth is found.

Gathered friends beneath the stars,
Laughter mingles with our scars.
Listen close as stories weave,
Together here, we all believe.

Sipping cider, spirits high,
Underneath the velvet sky.
Flickering flame, our hearts unite,
A festive pulse in the quiet night.

With each ember, dreams do spark,
A brightened path, dispelling dark.
United in joy, we share this night,
As fire's flicker brings delight.

The Thawing of Hearts

In wintry chill, the world does pause,
But springs forth warmth in love's sweet cause.
Beneath the surface, hearts awake,
The thawing whispers, no hearts to break.

Gentle breezes melt the ice,
Promising spring, like a soft device.
In gardens, buds begin to bloom,
Festive hues dispel all gloom.

Laughter flows through open doors,
Joyful reunions, as love restores.
Every hug a spark to start,
The dance of warmth, the thawing heart.

With every thaw, new hopes arise,
Underneath wide expansive skies.
In every smile, a promise shared,
The festive spirit, souls prepared.

The Dance of the Northern Lights

Auroras swirl in shades so bright,
A cosmic dance in the starry night.
Colors whisper across the sky,
Nature's canvas, a festal tie.

Glistening snow beneath our feet,
Each step reveals a wondrous feat.
Linked in awe, we gaze and sway,
As if the world comes out to play.

In every flash, our hearts take flight,
Together basking in the light.
A symphony both wild and free,
The dance of life, a jubilee.

Underneath this stunning sight,
We gather close, hearts shining bright.
In the magic of the night so grand,
A festive bond, together we stand.

Shadows Beneath the Pale Moon

The silver glow on frosted ground,
Whispers of joy in the night abound.
Laughter rises with the chilly breeze,
As shadows dance among the trees.

With lanterns flickering, hearts ignite,
Embracing warmth in the frosty night.
Each whispered secret, a festive cheer,
Beneath the moon, the glow is clear.

Songs of old fill the crisp air,
While friendships blossom, a moment rare.
Together we gather, smiles so bright,
In the shadows beneath the pale moonlight.

The world slows down in this magic hour,
Nature's beauty, a wondrous flower.
Hand in hand, we make our stand,
In the festival of dreams so grand.

Nature's Hibernation

Snowflakes whirl in a gentle dance,
Nature rests, caught in a trance.
Blankets of white on slumbering ground,
A peaceful hush, where dreams are found.

Branches cradle the soft, pure snow,
As winter whispers, time moves slow.
Crisp air carries the scent of pine,
In hibernation, all is divine.

Beneath the surface, life still thrives,
In hidden corners, warmth derives.
Nature awaits the sun's warm kiss,
In this stillness, we find our bliss.

So let us gather and lift our cheer,
In nature's arms, we hold so dear.
With hearts aglow in the winter's grace,
We celebrate life in this sacred space.

Crystalline Dreams in White

Glistening treasures on every tree,
Nature's art for all to see.
Each crystal shimmers in the light,
Creating dreams of pure delight.

Footprints trace a playful path,
In the midst of winter's laugh.
Children giggle, their spirits soar,
Building memories, evermore.

In frozen forests, whispers sound,
As magic dances all around.
The world is bright, a canvas wide,
In crystalline dreams, we take pride.

Under the stars, a festive air,
Hearts entwined, with love to share.
As night unfolds and candles gleam,
We bask together in this dream.

The Dance of Frozen Branches

Branches sway in the winter's chill,
As joy spreads wide, on the silent hill.
Snowflakes twirl in a delicate ballet,
Celebrating life in their own way.

The forest hums with a soft refrain,
Echoing peace through the frosty plain.
Nature's rhythm, a soothing sound,
In the dance of frozen branches, we're bound.

With every spark of the twilight's glow,
A festive spirit starts to grow.
Hands come together, laughter rings,
In the warmth that the frost still brings.

So let us sway in this wintry grace,
As snowflakes gather, we find our place.
Together we dance, hearts full of cheer,
In the magic of winter, we hold dear.

Echoes of Warmth in the Frost

In icy air, laughter rings,
Joyful voices, the heart sings.
Brightly lit, each window glows,
With every breath, the magic flows.

Chasing shadows, dancing light,
Turning cold to pure delight.
All around, the spirits cheer,
Together we spread warmth and cheer.

Snowflakes twirl in gentle grace,
Children's smiles in every place.
A tapestry of fleeting bliss,
Moments wrapped in warmth, we kiss.

In the frosty breath we find,
Echoes of love, intertwined.
Through whispered winds, the stories play,
A festive heart, forever stay.

Heartbeats Beneath the Surface

Beneath the snow, a rhythm beats,
Silent hopes in the cold retreats.
Awakening dreams in winter's keep,
Through hushed whispers, the earth does sleep.

Crystalline stars in a velvet sky,
We gather close, as time goes by.
With every cheer, our spirits rise,
In the glow of warmth, love never dies.

Candles flicker, casting gold,
Stories of wonder slowly unfold.
Hand in hand, the world feels right,
Together we embrace the night.

In every heartbeat, a spark ignites,
Under the frost, the love unites.
A festive air, a joyous treat,
In this moment, we are complete.

Frosty Soliloquy

In twilight's breath, the chill cascades,
Each frosty breath, a serenade.
Branches glisten, diamonds bright,
A soliloquy of silent night.

Whispers dance, each note so clear,
The magic of winter draws us near.
Echoes loop, with laughter spun,
Where shadows play, and dreams outrun.

Wrapped in warmth, we share our dreams,
Under the stars, the world redeems.
A festive heart, with love we gather,
In frosty whispers, our spirits chatter.

With every moment's soft embrace,
We savor joy in this sacred space.
In the frosty air, connections bloom,
Embraced by winter's gentle loom.

The Art of Winter's Palette

Colors swirl, a canvas bright,
Snowflakes paint, a pure delight.
Crimson berries, emerald trees,
Nature's art in every breeze.

On frosty panes, our breath will trace,
The sketches of love in every space.
With laughter shared, we find our way,
In winter's embrace, we choose to play.

Evenings twinkle with golden hue,
Gathering joy in all that we do.
Under the warmth of twinkling lights,
Every heart unites on winter nights.

With each brushstroke, memories blend,
A festive melody, we all send.
In the winter's art, we forever dwell,
The canvas of life, a timeless spell.

Twilight in the Tundra

The sun dips low, golden gleam,
A dance of light, a winter dream.
Snowflakes twirl, with joyful grace,
Nature's beauty, a warm embrace.

Stars emerge, the night takes flight,
The tundra sparkles, pure delight.
Warm hearts gather, laughter shared,
In this twilight, none are scared.

The icy air, a crisp delight,
Together, we chase away the night.
Fires crackle, stories flow,
In this moment, love will glow.

As dawn approaches, colors blend,
A festive spirit, never ends.
In the tundra, we find our tune,
Underneath the silver moon.

Ethereal Landscapes of White

A canvas bright, with shimmering snow,
Whispers of magic, where cool breezes blow.
Silver trees, dressed in light,
Beneath the stars, a wondrous sight.

Friends gather round, with hearts aglow,
As laughter rings, and spirits flow.
Every moment, a cherished trace,
In this white land, we find our place.

Delicate flakes, a ballroom dance,
Nature's beauty, invites a glance.
With every heartbeat, joy ignites,
In these landscapes, our hopes take flight.

The twilight sings, a gentle cheer,
In these white hills, we hold each dear.
Ethereal dreams wrapped in the night,
Together we shine, forever bright.

Nightfall in the Frozen Woods

The woods are hushed, a blanket white,
Stars above twinkle, a lovely sight.
Moonlight spills, like silver wine,
We gather close, hearts intertwine.

Each breath a cloud, the air so clear,
In this stillness, we have no fear.
Crackling branches, soft and slow,
Echoes of laughter, in the glow.

Frost-kissed trails lead us away,
Guided by moonbeams, come what may.
In the frozen arms of the night,
We find warmth, in shared delight.

As night deepens, shadows play,
In these woods, we dance and sway.
Together we stand, in this embrace,
Nightfall whispers, time and space.

Serenade of the Silent Willow

Beneath the willow, secrets weave,
A serenade, where dreams believe.
Gentle breezes beckon near,
The festive spirit we hold dear.

With lanterns lit, a warming glow,
Soft whispers dance, like falling snow.
Joyful hearts sway side by side,
In the stillness, love won't hide.

Under the stars, stories unfold,
Each moment treasured, pure as gold.
The willow sways, in soft delight,
Guarding dreams throughout the night.

As dawn breaks, colors embrace,
The serenade leaves a trace.
In the heart of the willow's song,
Festive echoes carry us along.

Echoes of the Gathering Storm

Laughter dances on the breeze,
Joyful hearts, the moment frees.
Together we weave tales so bright,
As storm clouds gather, igniting the night.

Colors splash across the sky,
Balloons drifting, soaring high.
Gather around, let the music bloom,
In this festival, joy dispels all gloom.

Through flickered lights and twinkling stars,
We sing to the rhythm of beating guitars.
The gathering storm, a thrilling embrace,
In every heart, we find our place.

Under the glow of lanterns warm,
We celebrate life, we weather the storm.
With every cheer and every toast,
Together we rise, this night we boast.

The Sigh of Snow-Covered Pines

Whispers of wonder in the air,
Pines draped in blankets, crystalline flare.
Children laughing, snowflakes twirl,
In this magic, worries unfurl.

Candles flicker with hopeful light,
Carols echo through the silent night.
The world is hushed, yet hearts are loud,
Dancing to joy, wrapped in a shroud.

Glistening paths of powdery white,
Every step a delight, pure and bright.
The sigh of pines, a gentle call,
In snowy dreams, we rise and fall.

Cocoa sipped by warm fireside,
Memories made, no need to hide.
In this festive scene, love expands,
Snow-covered Pines lend us their hands.

Shimmering Echoes of the North

Stars sprinkle magic on the snow,
Whispers of the North, gentle flow.
Fires crackle, warmth shared in a hug,
Under the sky, the world's a shrug.

Drifting with dreams, we carve our fate,
In shimmering echoes, we resonate.
Laughter spills like the wine we share,
With every toast, we lighten our care.

Northern lights dance, a cosmic show,
Glowing bright in the winter's glow.
Hand in hand, we twirl and spin,
In every moment, new hopes begin.

Time fades softly, yet hearts stay bold,
With tales of warmth, and love retold.
In shimmering echoes, we find our way,
Together we shine, in festive array.

Frosted Fields at Dusk

Golden hues fade into night,
Frosted fields, a joyous sight.
Children's laughter fills the air,
Winter's slumber, a moment rare.

Footprints mark where we have been,
A canvas blank, a world of sin.
Carols rise, the shadows play,
In frosted fields, we wish to stay.

Sparkling snow, a world reborn,
In every heart, the festive warm.
Together we dance in the chilling breeze,
Finding solace in moments like these.

As dusk settles, stars take their place,
In this quiet, we find our grace.
Frosted fields, where dreams take flight,
Together we bask in the warmth of light.